Wicca

The Ultimate Beginner's Guide to Learning Spells & Witchcraft

Sarah Thompson

Sarah Thompson

Disclaimer

All rights reserved. No part of this publication may be reproduced, distributed, or transmitted in any form or by any means, including photocopying, recording, or other electronic or mechanical methods, without the prior written permission of the publisher, except in the case of brief quotations embodied in critical reviews and certain other noncommercial uses permitted by copyright law.

Sarah Thompson

© **Copyright 2015 by Sarah Thompson - All rights reserved.**

This document is geared towards providing exact and reliable information in regards to the topic and issue covered. The publication is sold with the idea that the publisher is not required to render accounting, officially permitted, or otherwise, qualified services. If advice is necessary, legal or professional, a practiced individual in the profession should be ordered.

From a Declaration of Principles which was accepted and approved equally by a Committee of the American Bar Association and a Committee of Publishers and Associations.

In no way is it legal to reproduce, duplicate, or transmit any part of this document in either electronic means or in printed format. Recording of this publication is strictly prohibited and any storage of this document is not allowed unless with written permission from the publisher. All rights reserved.

The information provided herein is stated to be truthful and consistent, in that any liability, in terms of inattention or otherwise, by any usage or abuse of any policies, processes, or directions contained within is the solitary and utter responsibility of the recipient reader. Under no circumstances will any legal responsibility or blame be held against the publisher for any reparation, damages, or monetary loss due to the information herein, either directly or indirectly.

Sarah Thompson

Respective authors own all copyrights not held by the publisher.

The information herein is offered for informational purposes solely, and is universal as so. The presentation of the information is without contract or any type of guarantee assurance.

The trademarks that are used are without any consent, and the publication of the trademark is without permission or backing by the trademark owner. All trademarks and brands within this book are for clarifying purposes only and are the owned by the owners themselves, not affiliated with this document.

Table of Contents

INTRODUCTION 9

SECRET CHAPTER: FREE BONUS – "THE NEW AGE HANDBOOK" 11

CHAPTER ONE – HISTORY 13

CHAPTER TWO – DEMOGRAPHICS 19

CHAPTER THREE – ACCEPTANCE 21

CHAPTER FOUR – BELIEFS 23

CHAPTER FIVE – TRADITIONS 31

CHAPTER SIX – PRACTICES 39

CHAPTER SEVEN: BASIC PRINCIPLES AND LAWS 55

CONCLUSION 91

SECRET CHAPTER: FREE BONUS – "THE NEW AGE HANDBOOK" 93

CHECK OUT MY OTHER BOOKS 99

Sarah Thompson

Introduction

Wicca is one of those subjects that very few people actually understand. This is not due to anything other than the simple fact that people don't fully have all of the information that they require. Over the course of this book, the goal will be to dispel a lot of the misconceptions and myths that have come out over the years concerning this topic. The goal of this book is to educate the reader on the following topics.

- History of Wicca
- Some of the beliefs
- Traditions associated with Wicca
- Practices
- Acceptance of Wiccans among society

Sarah Thompson

Hopefully once you have read this book, you will have a better understanding of this subject and will see that in a lot of ways that wiccans are no different than the person living next door to you. The biggest problem with society and Wicca is the fact that there is a severe lack of understanding on the subject and people tend to fear what they do not understand.

Secret Chapter: Free Bonus – "The New Age Handbook"

Like I promised you before in this small chapter I will give you a free EBook as a gift of mine.

Are you looking for something more out of life? If so, you are not alone. Many people are today and find the solution in the New Age Movement.
The New Age movement adopts ideas from a number of different movements that emphasize spirituality and the spiritual conscious mind. The main idea is to enforce serenity of the mind.

A few years ago I began having major problems with both my career and my personal life. As a result, I was suffering from large amounts of stress that impacted my health. I knew I needed to find a way to empower myself but I just couldn't seem to do it. As time went on, the stress became worse and so did my health.

I knew I had to do something.

Sarah Thompson

That's when I decided I had to find a way to improve my life. I knew I owed it to myself and my family to get a handle on this once and for all!

What I discovered completely changed my life!

How did I do it?

I would love to share my secrets with you and my new special report on New Age does just that!

Click [here](#) to download the book for free.

Alternatively you can check out this link: https://mjgpublishing.leadpages.net/sarahthompson/

Chapter One – History

The history of Wicca is a blurry subject at best, but there are some truths that most historians would agree with. Wicca is a form of pagan beliefs that derived hundreds of years ago; although, it has been morphed into a modern day religion and has many different aspects from the ancient roots it once shared.

Historians do know that Wicca is based off an ancient, northern European pagan belief system that involved a Goddess and a horned God, her consort. While the Wiccan religion is a modern creation, some of the sources for the religion pre-date the Christian era by hundreds of years. However, most Wiccans will argue that their religion is not a direct descendent of the pagan religion. They see their religion as a modern reconstruction of the earlier beliefs.

There is a theory the Wiccan religion began with the Celts, but there is very little evidence to prove this theory. There are no written records of the forms of worship, and the belief system the Celts followed. Unfortunately, the written documents of the Celts during the time that Wicca is thought to have first flourished are biased and have a questionable historical worth at best.

The most historical account of Wicca is a book written by a British civil servant, Gerald Gardener. In 1939, he wrote that was initiated into a remaining Wiccan Coven and took the vows of secrecy. He then persuaded them to allow him to write a book in 1949. This book revealed a few of the key components of the Wiccan belief system and it discussed some of the horrors of persecution these religious followers faced throughout history. The book was titled High Magic's Aid.

He then added in numerous symbols, rituals, concepts, and elements that were imperative to the ceremonial magic of Wicca, and he added in concepts in order to flesh out the practices. These practices were long forgotten by then modern day's society, and he awoke the both the good and the bad that came along with the Wiccan belief system being revealed to the public again.

In 1954, he wrote Witchcraft Today in order to describe some more of the details about the Wiccan faith. He also added in more spells and craft secrets so that others could follow the religion. Then he wrote The Meaning of Witchcraft in order to reveal the history and the belief system of Wicca in Northern Europe.

According to Gerald Gardner, Wicca began way back in prehistory as a ritual that was associated with the hunt, fire, fertility, plants, tribal fertility, and the curing of diseases. The religion then developed into a religion that acknowledged a supreme deity, but realized that they were not able to understand this deity at the time. Instead, they decided to worship the gods that were underneath this supreme deity, known as the Goddess of Fertility and the God of the Hunt.

This religion then developed into a moon-based worship while the sun-based faith of the priests of the Druids developed into the dominant religion of the Celts. By that time, the Celts spread across Northern Europe, but they never formed a political entity throughout their spread. They remained many separate tribes that shared a common religion and culture.

The religion then survived the Saxon, Roman, and Norman invasions by 'going underground' in order to survive. Unfortunately, a major loss to members occurred during the Christian genocides that continued all the way into the eighteenth century. During this time, many of the beliefs and the rituals had been lost as they were unable to be recorded for fear of persecution. The covens had become so isolate during these times that they lost contact with one another and started to form separate belief systems.

The religion was then revived Gardner and others who took those surviving practices and belief systems and fleshed them out using material from other religions and spiritual sources. He stated that after he had written the first book, he was graced with numerous letters that announced there had been covens that had survived for many generations.

There are those that believe the Wiccan belief system did not have a continuous presence from the Celtic times to the modern day. They maintain that the current religious belief system was created using a few pieces of Celtic deity structures, beliefs, and celebratory days in order to create the backbone of the Wiccan religion.

The consensus is that the recent Wiccan religion became a mass movement in England during the 1950's and has rapidly become a new-age religion that is expanding at a furious rate throughout North American and Europe. With this expansion came an uprising of economic and personal attacks on the religion until the mid-1990s when the assaults on religious members slowly began to decline due to the popularity of the religion and the growing acceptance.

The Wicca that is currently practiced today is barely fifty years old at this point, and the techniques that are used are not entirely what the elders of Wicca practiced even thirty years beforehand.

Of course, the threads of what was are weaved into what is now. The idea of Wicca is to move forward into the future using the knowledge of the past and expounding on it. After all, what is a practice without getting better?

Sarah Thompson

Chapter Two – Demographics

The exact demographics for the number of people that associate with Wicca are an interesting breakdown. The first thing that makes this so interesting is that the exact number is hard to actually get a handle on. Between the U.K and the U.S., many people have estimated there are around 800,000 people that in one form or another associated with Wicca in one manner or another. In the United States alone, the number went from around 8,000 people that identified themselves as Wiccan to over 130,000 eleven years later in 2001. This alone has given rise to the popularity of Wicca and the immense number of people that are on a daily basis finding this as a great alternative to the many other traditional religions of the world.

Around 75% of the Wiccans that are in the United States are female with the rest being made up of males as would be the natural assumption. Wicca is also the largest non-christen faith with over 1500 of the airmen in the Air Force that identify themselves as being part of Wicca. The numbers in the U.K are a bit more cloudy as there is a little more of a muddling that occurs among those that proclaim themselves as being Wiccan as opposed to any of the other non-Christin faiths in the country. One of the areas that caused this muddling is the fact that often druids and Wiccans were tossed into the same category, as well as heathens. It is for this reason that getting the exact number of Wiccans in the U.K has been a bit of a tough job to nail down. There are methods that are being used to help and get an idea as to the number of Wiccans in the U.K.

In other parts of the world, the number of Wiccans is not as easy to determine as there is not a lot of record keeping done for Wicca as some countries are still looking at Wicca as a non-Christin faith that does not deserve to be acknowledged. While this thought process is slowly breaking down, it is unfortunately still at a point that a lot of non-believers are not eager to get on board and fully embrace this. The simple matter of truth is that we may never know the exact number of people who are associated with Wicca as there is not a reliable way of measuring this or there are simply a lot of people that prefer to hide from everyone else and keep this fact to themselves. The one thing that we do know for sure is that these numbers will, over time, continue to grow and we will see a big rise in the number of Wiccans.

Chapter Three – Acceptance

Acceptance of Wicca has been a long and drawn-out road to travel. While it has been made a little easier with the topic being part of our media, it has untimely been a very tough road. Even former President George Bush said that he did not believe Wicca was an actual religion. Many associated with the Wiccan faith have worked hard to get some form of legitimate acknowledgment on the subject. In the United States, there have been a number of legal cases that have helped to make the subject gain a little bit of respect from those that at one point may have been a non-believer.

There is, however, many in the faith community that will look at Wicca as a form of Satanism, even though, there are a large number of differences between these two types of religion. It is these beliefs that still to this day haunt those that are looking to get Wicca acknowledged as a real faith.

Sarah Thompson

It is also important that many that practice Wicca are still scared to come out to their friends and family. When one of these people make it difficult to actually come out, it is often referred to as "coming out of the broom closet." One of the main reasons why Wiccans are afraid to come out to their friends and family is that they are often looked at as being anti-Christian and, as a result, are not accepted as openly as some people might think they are. This is why a lot of Wiccans have made the decision to refrain from coming out and just make the decision to stay hidden and keep that part of their life private as opposed to coming out and facing being not accepted.

In Canada, the fight has been slightly easier and led to the first officially recognized Chaplin at a university. This has helped to open a lot of the doors that Wiccans have been able to go through and as such seen an increase in the amount of support in years past.

Chapter Four – Beliefs

Within the Wiccan world, there are a number of issues that tend to have differences among the many different traditions. There is however among certain topics a common school of thought that seems to be present. These topics are as such and will be expanded on in more detail in this chapter.

- Theology
- Afterlife
- Magic
- Morality
- Five elements

Theology

The aspect of a "god" can get a little clouded at times. The reason for this is that there is no common school of thought on this subject. This, in turn, leads to there being a dual thought that there is a horned god as well as a goddess. Many people that believe in Wicca will say that the goddess represents all that is the air, water, moon, stars, and earth. On the other side of things, the horned god will often represent that of the sun, forests, as well as the animals.

Some sections will see that there is just one deity that they will regard as being a goddess. While others will see that the deity is actually genderless. This all depends on which school of thought that you tend to go with in terms of your actual beliefs.

Afterlife

The concept of the afterlife is one that has a bit of varied schools of thought surrounding the topic. There is the underlying thought that the concept of reincarnation is the leading thought on this subject. This is a thought that goes all the way back to the 1930's with the New Forest Coven.

Behind this belief, the spirit of the person reincarnates over and over in an effort to learn many of the lessons that the world has to teach them. It is important to note that this thought is not universally accepted as there are many Wiccans that believe that the spirit will reincarnate into many different species over the course of time. It is also important that you know that many

Wiccans do not focus as much on the afterlife as much as they do in this current life that they are living.

Magic

Many people that are associated with Wicca will say that they believe in some form or another in the concept of magic.

It is first important to understand that magic is a universally accepted concept within the Wicca world. Many find this to be performed through the use of witchcraft or some form of sorcery. The main thought within the Wiccan community is that magic is a law of nature that has been very much misunderstood by science. This, in turn, has led many to not look at this subject as supernatural but rather part of the super powers that naturally reside in nature. This belief has led many that are associated with Wicca to look at the subject as being something that the universe is actually in control of and that they are mere vessels that aid in what the universe naturally tends to do.

When a Wiccan does perform magic, it is often part of a sacred circle and is referred to as a working as opposed to a spell. These are meant to bring about real changes in the physical world often to help benefit a person this is what it referred to as white magic as opposed to the magic associated with evil, which is called black magic. Some of the things that white magic can be used for is relationships, health, fertility, healing, protection or to banish negative energy out of a person's life.

There is a growing system that feels there should not be any color associated with either form of magic as they feel the term black being associated with evil is not a fair association to be made.

Morality

Within the Wiccan world, there is a very strong sense of ethics. This is contrary to what a large number of people actually think when the topic of Wicca comes up. There are those that think that Wicca is used as a way to get back at someone or to encourage harm to come someone's way. Actually, it's the opposite.

Many Wiccans take a "do no harm" approach toward their work. This comes from the fact that there is a moral ground that has to be considered and a certain level of responsibility for the actions that one takes with their Wicca comes with it. Another aspect that is present in Wicca is that the actions that a person performs, good or bad, will return to them triple. This is often known as the threefold return. This is another reason why there are often a lot of positive things that are associated with Wicca as opposed to doing negative work.

There is also a set of eight virtues that generally are looked at many Wiccans as worth being cultivated in their day to day life.

These eight virtues are as follows: mirth, reverence, honor, humility, strength, beauty, power and compassion. The overall goal for a true Wiccan is to find a way in their day to day life to take these and expand on them in their life.

Five Elements

Another important part of the Wiccan belief system is that of the five elements. These consist of air, fire, water, earth and spirit. Spirit is looked at as the glue that connects the other four to one another. It is also often a common thought that each of the four is associated with that of a direction. South is associated with fire, air is associated with the east, water is associated with the west and earth is generally associated with the north.

It a common misconception that each person who practices Wicca is associated with an element, and while many believe that there is an element they are more apt to resonate with, all Wiccans strive to work with all five elements. Therefore, it is imperative to use the five different elements when performing any ritual in order to achieve balance. Wicca is, after all, about universal balance.

Read further for more information about the different elements of Wicca.

Earth

Earth is considered the most feminine element out of all the elements and is associated with the North. It is a fertile, stable element that is most associated with the Goddess. The earth element is associated with the actual planet earth and is about all that is contained on the planet, nature, and life. It is about the different aspects of life: birth, life, death, and rebirth. This is a nurturing, stable, solid, firm, enduring, and strong element.

The colors associated with this element are brown and green in all their forms.

Air

Air is very deeply connected to the soul and the breath of life. It is associated with the direction East. Most Wiccans focus on this element when they are doing a ritual that focuses on wisdom, communication, and the mind. This element brings in positive thoughts and blows away the strife and negative aspects of one's life.

It is associated with the colors white and yellow in all their shades.

Fire

Fire is the most masculine element and is associated with purification. Its direction is south and is strongly connected with a strong will and energy. This element is known to both create and destroy and is a symbolization of the horned God. It can both heal and harm and it can bring about new life or destroy old and worn life.

Its colors are orange and red in all their shades.

Water

Water is also considered a feminine element and is connected to the Goddess. Its direction is west, and it is used for purification, cleansing, and healing. Water is associated with emotions and passion, and it's not only used in Wicca. Water has been used in almost every religion around the world for purification purposes, so the theme is very strong. Water can be used to consecrate tools and the circle before a Wiccan ritual.

The colors of water are all the shades of blue.

Spirit

Spirit is the element that binds the other four elements together. It is the prime element, representing all the connections and space in order for the other elements to exist. It is an essential element to the feelings of togetherness for the coven and represents the sense of union, joy, transcendence, change, transformation, and immanence. Spirit is the representation of the human soul and the God and Goddess together. The direction associated with spirit is a complete lack of direction and dimension.

Colors associated with the element spirit are black, white, and purple.

Chapter Five – Traditions

There are a large number of traditions that are associated with Wicca that many people might not even know existed. These traditions are the heart and soul of what makes Wicca and has been a part of the religion for as long as it has been recorded in history. In this chapter, we will look at a few of these traditions. The first of these traditions is that of the coven.

The coven is one of the most basic of traditions that is associated with Wicca. One of the traditions that are associated with a coven is that the number of members is usually around thirteen. This number can in cases be larger or smaller. When a coven exceeds the ideal number, it is what is called hived. This means that the coven has broken off on its own but is still part of the group. When you have a group of hives, you have what is called a grove of members.

To become a part of a coven will generally involve a period of study that will last one year and a day. This time can involve a set course of study to ensure that the person looking to join the coven has been given the proper amount of education to know all about Wicca and the many aspects that surround it.

It is also important to know that many people associated with Wicca may have many schools of thought that they fall in line with. This means that in the end, you can have what is often called eclectic Wicca. While some will look at this as a total abandonment of the Wiccan faith, it is in other circles looked at as a mere expansion of one's perception and allows them the chance to exceed their limitations.

The more that a person dives into the world of Wicca and all of the practices that are associated with it, the important thing to keep in mind is that these traditions while a part of Wicca are not set in stone and often will mean that there is some room for expansion.

Here are some different Wiccan traditions and how they derived so that you may have a better idea of what tradition you may want to join.

Gardnerian Wicca

Perhaps one of the most popular traditions of Wicca is the Gardnerian Wicca, created by Gerald Gardner in 1951 with the publication of his book on the craft. He was one of the first to go public with his practice of the religion and became a figurehead of the resurgence of the tradition. This tradition or sect of Wicca has a strong resemblance to pagan beliefs as the practitioners have a strong affiliation with nature, colorful rituals, and a deliberate challenge to conventional society and religion. For example, many Gardnerian Wicca practitioners will practice what is known as sky-clad or nude.

Those who wish to join a Gardnerian Wiccan coven must be initiated into the coven and cannot initiate themselves. There is a structured system in which the initiates learn about the religion.

Alexandrian Wicca

Alex Sanders dubbed himself the King of witches and founded his tradition of Wicca in the 1960s in England. Many of his beliefs and rituals are based on the Gardnerian Wicca traditions. He insisted on a coven and members only being allowed to attend meetings, and he insisted on nude meetings. The Alexandrians place more emphasis on ceremonial magic with some Judeo-Christian elements.

Seax Wicca

Also known as Saxon Wicca, Seax Wicca was founded in the United States in 1973 by Raymond Buckland, who was an original follower of the Gardnerian Wicca tradition under Gerald Gardner. He moved to the United States in 1962 and decided to move away from some of the practices of the Gardnerian Wicca covens. For instance, he determined that covens could choose whether or not to work nude or robed, and that witches could be imitated through self-study or through a coven.

British Traditional Wicca

The British Traditional Wiccans have a belief system that either resonates with Gerald Gardner's system or the Janet and Stewart Farrar practices. They are highly structured groups who have neophytes or beginners that follow a degree program, much like the Gardnerian, and they tend to mix the Gardnerian and Celtic traditions together.

Georgian Wicca

In this Wiccan tradition, diversity is encouraged and the practitioners will come up with their own rituals in order to fulfill a need. Some will work nude while others will work fully clothed, and some will work alone or in a coven. George Patterson founded the tradition in 1970 in Bakersfield, California.

Algard Wicca

Established in 1972 by Mary Nesnick, this combination of the Gardnerian and Alexandrian tradition is very similar to the Gardnerian Wicca traditions.

Druidic Wicca

Many argue that this is not really a tradition of Wicca, but historians classify it as such. It takes the Druidic and Celtic belief systems and mixes them with the healing powers of minerals and plants, as well as the beliefs of faeries, gnomes, and elemental spirits. This tradition of Wicca uses Gardnerian rituals but stresses nature, the elements, and the Ancient Ones.

Reclaiming Wicca

Found in 1980 by Starhawk in the San Francisco Bay area, this tradition was based on the Feri tradition from Victor Anderson. However, this tradition has more of a focus on the linking of magic and spirituality with some political activism. While this no longer exists, the tradition still thrives. It's a non-hierarchical tradition and many members attend week-long 'witch camps' in Canada, the United States, Germany, and England.

Dianic Wicca

This tradition is named after the Greek goddess Diana and focuses on the Goddess while it softens the role of the God. Founded by Zsuzsanna Budapest in the 1970s, this is largely a feminist movement within the Wiccan traditions. The Goddess is worshiped as the Maiden, Mother, and the Crone. Most covens only welcome women and ostracize men, but there are some with this tradition that do welcome men.

Blue Star Wicca

This is based mostly on the Alexandrian tradition and is a collection of covens that began in the '70s in Pennsylvania. It has since spread across the United States due to the members traveling through the country as musicians and spreading their ideas.

Black Forest Clan

This tradition accepts the Druidic, Celtic, German, and Gardnerian traditions and prepares a practitioner to go on to become part of the Wiccan clergy as a licensed High Priest or High Priestess. These practitioners then go on to make their own covens, keeping the clan strong in unity and numbers.

Lothlorien Wicca

This is an earth-based tradition that has its roots in Wicca and other religions of the world. This tradition celebrates the cycles of life and the seasons. It is accepting of all people regardless of their ethnicity, culture, socioeconomic status, sexual orientation, or religion. It was founded in 1977 by Reverend Paul Beyerl, who was a neo-Alexandrian initiate.

Eclectic Wicca

This is a growing belief system or tradition of Wicca that states that those who wish to practice Wicca do not need to go through an initiate process in order to practice the craft. They discard the institutions of traditional Wicca and have wider beliefs that are less strictly observed. Some of them do not perform rituals and do not identify as a witch. They can be solitary or work in covens, and they outnumber the traditional initiates of traditional Wicca.

Solitaires

A branch of the Eclectic Wiccans, Solitaires are solitary practitioners. They may attend community events and gatherings, but they reserve their spiritual practices and rituals for when they are alone.

Sarah Thompson

Chapter Six – Practices

When talking about practices that are associated with Wicca, there are a number of these that an average person might not otherwise have been made aware of should books like this one to have come out. One thing that needs to be remembered is that many of these practices take place on a full moon as this time seems to hold a lot of importance in the world of Wicca.

There are also a lot of tools that are associated with casting many of the spells that are performed within a circle. These tools often include the use of a knife, a wand, a pentacle as well as a chalice. There are other tools that might be uses such as a broomstick that is also known as a besom, candles, incense as well as a caldron. These tools are all part of the process of performing magic and casting a number of the spells that you will come across while looking into Wicca.

One of the common misconceptions that seem to be associated with Wicca is that a lot of people practice in the nude. This is a tradition that does occur that is also known as skyclad. This is not the typical way that many members practice as they will go with a more traditional means of practice. Some people that practice does so with a robe and a rope tied around their middle.

The wheel of the year is a term that is given to the many of the celebrations that take place throughout the year. These are often referred to as Sabbaths; there are traditionally around eight Sabbaths that Wiccans tend to celebrate throughout the year. Some clans will observe six of these while others will observe four of these to fall in line with that of the four seasons that are celebrated.

For a person to join a coven, it is a process that has three stages and can vary in the amount of time needed. This will depend greatly on the person that is looking to join as well as those that are part of the initiation process. Some have said that this process can take as little as six months while others claim that it can take as long as a year to become part of Wicca.

Weddings are held in the Wiccan faith and are generally referred to as hand fasting ceremonies'. In a handfasting ceremony the "till death do us part" is replaced with a more traditional "for as long as love lasts."

Infants go through a process known as Wiccaning. This is the Wicca same as that of a christening. The purpose of this is designed to present the infant to the god and goddess for protection.

Tools

There are many fundamental tools to the average Wiccan that is looking to practice the art of having an altar and performing rituals.

Athame

The athame is a ritual knife and is one of the most important altar tools. The athame is a traditionally black-handled tool that is set to the east of the altar, and represents thoughts, the mind, and choice. A common misconception is that the athame has to be metal, but in reality, it doesn't. There are many that are made from wood or stone because they are not used as a physical knife but as a symbolic representation of a knife.

The athame holds the God energy or the yang energy and is used in order to direct energy. It is the main tool used to cast a circle and recall a ritualistic circle. They are rarely if ever, used to cut anything on the physical plane.

Bell

The bell is a representation of the Goddess' Voice. When it's rung, it is supposed to bring the Divine's attention to the ringer and the ringer's attention to the Divine. A bell with a beautiful tone can call healing energy to the ringer, and if the unwanted energy comes about during a ritual, the ringer can dispel the energy using the bell.

Direction Candles

As you've most likely guessed, the direction candles are physical representations of the cardinal directions. They are usually color-coded and used on the altar. The northern candles are usually green, brown, or black. The eastern candles are usually white or yellow. The southern candles are orange or red. The west candles are aqua or blue, and the center candles are representations of the God and Goddess. These candles are usually silver, white, or gold, or a combination.

God and Goddess Candles

These candles are usually pillar candles and are used in order to represent the God and Goddess. They're set on either side of the Pentacle toward the center of the altar. Some other alterations of this are setting out three candles, one white, one red, and one black for the Maiden, Mother, and Crone. However, there are some alternative placements if the candles might drip on something that is delicate or catch something on fire. Always go with safety first.

Chalice

The chalice is a physical representation of the mother Goddess and is the yin of the altar tools. Some prefer a bejeweled cup for their chalice, but it's not necessary. Any cup or wine glass will do, or even a bowl. Anything that holds water and is round and curvy is a great representation of the Mother Goddess.

Silver a great choice of color for a chalice as this represents the Goddess, too. Chalices are used in order to offer libations to the Divine, hold water-water solutions, or as a ceremonial drinking tool. The chalice should be placed to the west.

Deities

An image or a representation of the god and goddess that are special to you are always great additions to the altar; however, they are not really considered altar tools. They are a reminder that the Divine is with you and they hold the vibrations of the Divine. Therefore, the altar becomes a living temple where the Divine dwells.

Libation Dish

The libation dish is a small bowl, cup, or dish that goes in the center of the altar in order to receive any offerings to the God or

Goddess. You can also use the altar chalice or a caldron for this purpose. You should pour or bury the libations into the Earth or in running water such as a river or stream to carry them off to the Divine.

Pentacle

The pentacle is a five-point star that is held within a circle and is placed in the center of the altar. The pentacle is also considered one of the most important altar tools as it offers protection and power in magical works. It is not to be confused with a pentagram.

Salt Water

Salt water is a staple to almost any religious group across the globe. A small bowl of salt water is used for cleansing and should be placed in the center. The altar chalice can be used to hold the salt water.

In Wicca, salt and water are both purifying elements not only the physical realm, but in the energetic realm, too. It also represents the energies of water and earth united and represents the ocean's womb that gave birth to all life on this planet.

Incense or Feather

Incense or a feather can be used in order to represent air. These go in the east in order to represent air, and the sacred scents can be used in order to cleanse an area energetically.

Crystals or Stones

Crystals or stones can be put in the northern part of the altar in order to represent earth. They each bring different types of energies to the altar, so I recommend that you choose wisely and look up the energies associated with these crystals or stones before you place them on the altar. Gemstones can carry certain energies to the altar.

Wand

The wand is a portable version of the broom and there is a theory that there was one instrument that performed both the wand and the broom's rituals long ago. A wand is able to be made of any natural material, but wood is traditional. Since all of them have a unique power, you may want to look up the meaning of the wood your wand was carved from and choose wisely.

Wands are often used for divination and channeling magical energy. They can also be used to cast or recall a circle in place of an athame.

The wand should go to the south for willpower, transformation, and magic. The wand also represents the yang or God energy.

Rituals

There are many different rituals for Wiccans, but let's start with some beginner ones. These rituals are often used by Wiccans, so they are good ones to memorize or at least write down in your book of shadows.

Water Blessing

Many keep a chalice of water on their altar, and this water is blessed in order for it to be pure. This dispels any negative energy that could interfere with any further rituals. You want to obtain water that is from a spring, but tap water can do just fine in a pinch.

Blessing water is very simple. Just put one hand over the water and say a prayer over the water. An example of a prayer might be:

Divine Mother and Father, purify this water with your powers and blessed be.

At this point, you want to add a little salt to the water to purify it, or insert a pentacle or a blessed athame into the chalice of water.

Blessed water can be used in order to prepare a position, purify another tool, or protect against negative entities. When you need to replace the water, do not pour it down the drain. Show some respect and use it as an offering to a tree outdoors or to a potted, indoor plant.

Altar Consecration

Once you have an altar set up and all the pieces of it are blessed, you may want to perform an altar consecration ritual. This ritual will protect your altar from negative energies and allow you to bring the God and Goddess's blessings upon the altar.

Once you've found a spot, use a smudge wand of sage and clear the air around the area you will set up the altar. Be sure to think calming, peaceful thoughts as you move to the four elements and ask for their presence and guidance. Use a compass if you need to find the proper directions.

Put a candle at each of the four directions and light the candle in a circle around the altar. You want to put a yellow candle to the east, a red candle to the south, a blue candle to the west, and a green candle to the north. Bless them in that order.

Then, set up the altar by placing the items you'd like to add to the altar and charge them as you go along. Once the altar is set up the way you'd like it, meditate a few moments and send healing and positive energy toward the altar.

Now, feel the magic and energy of the God and Goddess and dedicate the sacred space to them. Once you're ready to end the ritual, thank the elements for their assistance and thank the God

47

and Goddess for their presence. Then take a deep breath and repeat:

So mote it be, it is done.

Self-Purification

You may want to perform this ritual before you perform any other rituals at your altar. If you bring negative energy to the altar, you will taint your rituals with it. Therefore, fast the day before a ritual, purify yourself with a smudge purification of sage and meditate before you perform a ritual.

Ritual Space Purification

Before you begin a ritual at your ritual space, you may want to purify it. If you are using an indoor space, physically clean it thoroughly. If you are using an outdoor space, remove any rocks or sticks you may step on and clear the space as best you can. Then, take your ritual broom and clean the astral garbage in the area and the psychic clutter.

Casting a Circle

When you're finally sure the area is clean of any psychic or physical debris, you'll want to open up a circle in order to invite the powers of the God and Goddess to your performance. Everyone has a specific ritual that they perform in order to cast their circle, and each casting of the circle can be different. You'll want to go with what feels right.

First, set the boundary with cords, seal it with water, incense, salt, and a candle. Call the four quarters, and then call on the God and Goddess. The circle is meant to protect you from harm, so ask for their blessing and their understanding before you begin.

The Ritual

Rituals can be a celebration of the Sabbats, spell work, meditation, or a ritual of thanks to the deities. Energy is sent toward a goal, and a simple feast usually follows. Use your instincts when performing a ritual to make it personal and make it more powerful.

Closing a Circle

You'll want to first thank the God and Goddess for their time and their presence, and then the guardians of the four quarters. The circle should be sucked back up into the athame. Again, do what feels right and be respectful of all the tools and materials you used during your ritual. Throw nothing in the garbage or down the drain. Instead, discard of anything you may have used back to nature.

Observances

Just like many other religions across the globe, Wicca celebrates the Wheel of the Year, or the cycle of birth, death, and rebirth. Each of the spokes on this wheel, eight in total, represent a Sabbat.

The Sabbats are as follows.

Samhain (October 31st)

Samhain is the Witches' New Year and the Last Harvest. It is known by many different names depending on the culture, but the representation of the holiday remains the same. Samhain is about honoring the ones who are no longer living and is about the veil of the living and the dead world becoming thin so that we may make contact with the ones we love.

It is a good time to contemplate the natural cycle of life and death, and it marks the end of summer. Samhain rituals are usually performed at a cemetery in order to honor the dead. It is important that you receive permission from the dead before you begin a ritual as it can go very wrong.

Yule (Winter Solstice, Around December 22nd)

Yule marks the return of the light and is considered one of the lesser Sabbats. It is about the Goddess giving birth to the God and divine babies being born on the day. It is a day where one should think about reincarnation, the cycle of life, and fertility.

The Yule tree is decorated with many decorations on this day, and the Yule log is burned. The mistletoe is hung and wreaths are draped in order to represent the circle of life. The Goddess will sleep after this day until Imbolc when she is said to come back as a young Maiden.

Imbolc (February 2nd)

Imbolc is a great Sabbat and represents the Goddess awakening from her long winter nap. It is a time for plotting, planning, and initiations. It is a celebration of the coming of the light.

Ostara (March 21st)

Ostara is a less Sabbat and marks the spring equinox. It is the holiday of fertility and is often associated with Easter because the decorating of eggs and the bunny are actually Pagan beliefs. The basket full of eggs represents the womb full of fertility.

It is a time to celebrate courtship and the union between the God and the Goddess. Most spend time in nature to recognize this holiday.

Beltane (May 1st)

Beltane is May Day and is another fertility holiday. The dancing around the phallic maypole is a tradition that is still carried out today. This Sabbat is the union between the God and the Goddess and fertility has burst forth from the Earth and the greenery is quickly returning. This is a fire festival that is celebrated by people jumping over fires in order to signify contact with the sun. The rituals are carried out in order to bless the crops for a bountiful harvest.

Litha (June 21st)

This is the Summer Solstice and is a great time for a bonfire to promise a bountiful harvest. This is the time when the energies of the Goddess magic are at their peak, and the Goddess is represented as a pregnant, joyous mother. Immerse yourself in nature with the fruits of the God and the Goddess.

Lughnasadh (August 1st)

A greater Sabbat, Lughnasadh is the first of the three harvest holidays. The work of spring and summer is finally beginning to pay off with the first harvests. You should make offerings of bread to the faery folk and wild animals at this time, and honor the pregnant Goddess by leaving libations.

Mabon (September 22nd)

Mabon is the Autumn Equinox and is the middle of the harvest. This is the celebration of nature's harmony and the balance of the

God and Goddess through the balance of night and day. It is a time to reap what you have sown, both psychically and physically.

The Goddess is heavily pregnant with the God at this time and leaving another libation or leaving an offering of wine is appropriate at this time.

Sarah Thompson

Chapter Seven: Basic Principles And Laws

The Four Elements are Part of All Magic

In Wicca there are five elements that govern all of life. Four of them are physical and the fifth is Spirit, intangible but always present. The Pentacle, or the five pointed star that is synonymous with Wicca, is based on the five elements. The points on the star correspond to elements.

The four physical elements are Earth, Air, Fire and Water. Each of these elements has different properties and traits. Whenever you perform a spell you will call upon each element in order to gain power for the spell. Your altar should contain at least one item representing each element.

Earth is represented by the color brown, stones and rocks, or actual earth.

Air is represented by the color yellow, feathers, and incense.

Water is represented by the color blue, seashells or seaglass, and fish.

Fire is represented by the color red, wood or ash, and flames.

Each element has a wide range of emotions, intentions, and properties associated with it. Learning to use and call upon the elements is an important part of learning how to be a practicing witch.

The Law of Intention

The Law of Intention states that your spell will be more influenced by the intention in your heart than the words that you say. So whenever you cast a spell you should be prepared to deal with whatever happens as a result of your intention. Many witches will meditate on a particular spell before performing it to make sure that their intention is positive before doing the spell.

Sometimes spells can have unintended consequences, and if you perform a spell with less than honorable intentions you may still have to deal with negative Karma and a solid hit of negative energy from the Law of Threefold Return. Once you perform a spell you can't take it back, so it is a good idea to know your intention before doing a spell.

That means that you have to have a little self-awareness, which you can develop through meditation. You should always be calm and clear headed when you cast a spell. Never cast a spell when you are angry or irritated because that could bleed through into the spell and totally change the intention that you are directing outward. A good way to prepare for spellcasting is to meditate, take a ritual bath, and be well rested before you begin.

Take Responsibility for Your Own Spells

Whether you are writing your own spells or performing spells that were written by someone else you have to be responsible for your own spells. The intent of the spell and the action that results from it are your responsibility. Spells are nothing to play with. That's why it's important not to perform spells that will hurt or manipulate another person.

Sarah Thompson

Spells rarely work in the way that you think they will. When you perform a spell what you think will happen is often not what happens. That's because once you put your energy and intention into the world the Universe will pick it up and run with it. But you are still responsible for whatever happens.

If you cast a spell and the result is good then by the Law of Threefold Return you will profit in some way from the spell. But if you perform a spell that is designed to hurt, manipulate, or harm someone else you will have to deal with the consequences of that spell.

When you are performing spells the intention that you put into the spell is just as important as the words you use in the spell. So if you say positive words in the spell but have a harmful intention when you cast the spell any harm that comes from the spell is your responsibility.

All Religions are Valid

Wiccans don't believe that Wicca is the only valid religion. Wiccans respect the beliefs of all people. They respect the religions from Ancient times and they respect the beliefs of people today. A lot of witches have beliefs that have been borrowed from other religions and mixed into one individualized faith.

Wiccans have a deep respect for the choice of all people to worship as they want, or not to worship if they don't want to. Since Wicca stresses individuality and personal responsibility most witches feel that they don't have to right to judge or condemn anyone else's faith.

Practicing Wicca is really a way to connect yourself to the flow of life, and witches think that doing anything to halt that flow or stand in the way of that connection like judging others is a waste of time.

If you want practice Wicca check your judgement at the door and be open to all faiths and all religious practices. Respect the beliefs of others the way that you want them to respect yours. That is the Wiccan way.

Sarah Thompson

Faith is Personal

You have noticed by now that there is a lot of emphasis on individuality in Wicca. That's because Wiccans believe that faith is personal. Your relationship with the divine should be one that you choose and one that you maintain because you want to, not because you are told you have to. Wiccans choose to follow the magical path because they are strong, independent, free thinkers who want to express faith in their own way. When you practice Wicca everything becomes deeply spiritual. You see magic and harmony all around you.

That's why spells are really acts of prayer. Just like meditation can be prayerful because it strengthens your connection to the Universal flow of energy. Developing a personal moral code and a strong connection to the Universe is something that Wiccans do because they want to live on their own terms and Wicca supports and celebrates that. No witch believes exactly the same things as another witch yet they recognize that they are all part of the same Universe.

Give Reverence to Ancestors

Wiccans believe that the cultures and people who came before have a lot to teach and should be acknowledged. Both personal and cultural ancestors are looked at with respect and honored at feasts. Wiccans believe that much of the knowledge and wisdom passed on from generation to generation is what makes it possible for Wicca to exist today. A lot of the magical lore and knowledge from the past is studied and used today in modern Wicca.

Wiccans often will include their ancestors when they give thanks to the deities not because they think their ancestors are gods and goddesses but because they believe that their ancestors were wise and powerful.

Wiccans also believe that the elderly should be venerated and respected for their knowledge and life experience. The Crone, which is one of the faces of the Goddess, celebrates the wisdom and power that come with age.

There is No Sin

Sometimes people raised in monotheistic religions have trouble accepting this Wiccan belief. Wiccans don't believe in sin. Sin as it exists in the Bible means "missing the mark" or acting in ways that don't honor God. But Wiccans don't believe in a single omniscient and omnipotent god. So, they don't believe that any action is an action that doesn't honor god. Sin is a concept that was created in the Bible so only people who follow the Bible believe in sin.

That doesn't mean Wiccans believe you can do whatever you want with no consequences. But it means that Wiccans don't believe in original sin, or that they will get punished by God for their actions. As a Wiccan you are responsible for your own actions and you don't have to answer to anyone but yourself for your actions. If you don't act responsibly then you will have to face Karma and The Law of Threefold Return but the choice of how you act is always up to you.

It might seem that witches are free to cause whatever havoc they want but if you have ever had to take responsibility for something you did that hurt someone you know that in some cases no punishment can be as bad as the punishment you give yourself. Taking true responsibility for your actions isn't always easy or fun. But Wiccans believe that personal responsibility is the price for personal choice.

Karma Exists

Wiccans also believe in Karma. Karma is similar to the Law of Threefold Return but it's different in that Karma includes intention. The Law of Threefold Return states that any energy you put out will return to you three times as strong. Karma states that your intentions as well as your actions will dictate the kind of future that you will have. If you have bad intentions and deliberately hurt people in order to get an advantage for yourself then you can expect bad or hurtful things to happen to you.

If you treat people with kindness and go out of your way to help them then you can expect good things to happen to you. Even though there is no doctrine or dogma in Wicca the Law of Threefold Return and Karma make it pretty clear that it's a bad idea to do bad things or try to hurt people. So most Wiccans make it a point to try and live a responsible and ethical life where they are kind to people, animals, and the planet as well being kind to themselves.

Wiccans don't believe in a devil or some figure that will dispense punishment but they know that there must be balance in the world. In order to keep that balance people who act in ways that hurt the environment, animals, or other people will have the same types of actions happen to them. And people who treat the environment, animals and other people with love and kindness can expect good things to happen to them. Cultures around the world and throughout history believe in Karma because they have seen it in action. You have probably seen Karma working in your own life at some point.

Astrology is a Valuable Divination Tool

Astrology isn't just a fun distraction to Wiccans. Astrology is a valued divination tool that can be used to help identify problems and patterns and suggest future events. Many Wiccans use Astrology and spend a lot of time learning how to correctly use Astrology as a divination tool.

Astrology is a science that has been used for thousands of years. In the Ancient World people spent decades studying Astrology in order to be able to predict world events and individual fortunes. Today Astrology isn't taken seriously by the public at large but Wiccans know this ancient science has played a huge role in magic and worship in every culture that ever lived.

Some Wiccans spend years studying Astrology in order to become more skilled at using it to divine the future. Astrology is a complicated science and it takes a lot of study in order to master it. Astrology is mainly taught from one person to another and not by courses in a school or educational method. If you want to delve more deeply into Astrology you can try to become an apprentice to an Astrologer and learn more about this mystical science.

Spirit Communication is real

Wiccans believe that some souls do get trapped on Earth and that it is possible to communicate with them. Using various methods Wiccans can try to contact these souls and help them cross over to the Summerland. Sometimes souls are trapped because of violence or fear. Other souls choose to stay close to the people that they loved during life. These souls can sometimes communicate a lot of insight to the people on Earth.

Wiccans believe in honoring and respecting these lost souls and helping them cross over whenever possible. This doesn't mean that they believe every claim of a haunting or paranormal activity is true. It just means that Wiccans accept the possibility of spirit communication and the possibility that spirits can interact with the physical human world.

One of the most common ways to interact with the spirits is a Ouija board or spirit board. Spirit boards were first used widely during the Spiritualism movement at the turn of the 20th century when millions of people believed in spirit communication and used the boards often to try and contact the souls of their deceased loved ones.

There Is No Heaven or Hell

Wiccans don't believe in heaven or hell. They believe in being responsible for your actions and casting spells responsibly and in the Law of Threefold Return. But they don't believe that deities punish people or reward them after death. There is no doctrine about an afterlife in Wicca. Most Wiccans believe in reincarnation, or that they will be reborn after they die. Reincarnation is a path to spiritual enlightenment so Wiccans believe that they will be reborn into another life based on the spiritual lessons they have yet to learn. They study and meditate to achieve as much enlightenment as possible so that when they are reborn they will not have to repeat the lessons they have already learned.

It can be hard for some people to let go of the ideas of eternal reward or eternal punishment but many people find it is more comforting and empowering to embrace the idea that each person is responsible for their actions in this life and that living ethically is its own reward. If you're a free thinker who has always believed in taking responsibility for your own actions the lack of dogma in Wicca could be a perfect fit for you.

Wiccans believe that before a soul is reincarnated it rests in the Summerland.

The Summerland is For Everyone

Before a soul is reincarnated it rests in the Summerland, according to Wiccan beliefs. The Summerland is different for everyone, and it is a place of rest and joy. When a person dies their soul resides in the Summerland before the soul is reborn to learn more spiritual lessons.

The Summerland might sound like heaven, but in the Wiccan faith everyone goes to the Summerland after they die. Even people who are bad or wicked will go the Summerland to wait for reincarnation. People who were not good people will not be punished. They just have to repeat the same lessons over and over again until they move to a new spiritual level. The Summerland is very personal and Wiccans believe that the experience of the Summerland is different for everyone. For one person the Summerland might resemble their beloved childhood home. For another it might resemble a tropical vacation.

Some souls get stuck or lost and don't arrive at the Summerland right away. Souls that are the victims of extreme violence or souls that are clinging to their human lives end up trapped on Earth and they can't go to the Summerland until they resolve the issues surrounding their deaths. Those souls are the ghosts that places, objects and people.

Priests and Priestesses Are There to Guide

Even though Wicca is a religion that has no hierarchy there are Wiccan priests and priestesses. But, they are not officially sanctioned by any council or hierarchy. Within a coven a priest and priestess will be chosen to play the role of the Horned God and the Goddess of the Moon during Sabbat ceremonies. Coven members may take turns playing these roles or it may be the same priest and priestess each time.

Priests and priestesses are Wiccans who have spent years studying magic, casting spells, and studying other topics like herbology, aromatherapy, divination and many more. They are given their titles by the other members of the coven because they learned in the ways of Wicca. Anyone can become a priest or priestess if they put in the time and effort to advance their skills.

Some covens may not have priests or priestesses because they are not required in Wicca. But some covens prefer to have the wisest and most educated witches in the group act as the priest and priestess to guide and counsel the other members of the coven.

No Weekly Worship Required

Most people think that in order to be part of a religion you need to attend some type of service every week but Wicca doesn't require that. Wiccans revere the Earth, so holding a service inside a building doesn't make much sense. Wiccans are also guided by the Lunar cycle, not the weekly calendar. There is no weekly service required in Wicca. If you join a coven then the coven may get together weekly for spells or studying or even just socializing but it's not required.

You don't need to join a coven or even have other Wiccan friends in order to practice Wicca. It helps to have some people who share your beliefs in your life but it's really not necessary. You can be a successful Wiccan all by yourself if that is what is comfortable to you. Many people like to join covens because of the shared beliefs and camaraderie but if you are a person that prefers to be alone you can be a solitary witch.

Sarah Thompson

Coven activities can include everything from spell work and rituals on Sabbats to friendly pot lucks and picnics. If you are new to Wicca joining a coven will give you a whole network of knowledgeable friends to help you develop your own magic powers. So if there is a coven in your area you might want to think about joining, although you don't have to in order to practice magic.

No Rites of Passage Necessary

Most religions require that people go through several rites of initiation in order to become full members. Usually the first step it baptism and then there are other rites like confirmation or even marriage. But there are no official initiation rites in Wicca. You can get started right away and you don't have to prove yourself in any way. If you join a coven later on you may need to go through some type of imitation that is set by the coven but if you want to be a solitary practitioner you don't need anyone's approval.

That's because there is no official hierarchy in Wicca. Some other religions are structured in such a way that people need to go through a priest or pastor in order to be connected to a deity. But Wicca is all about building a personal relationship with the divine so you don't need anyone but yourself to practice Wicca. There's no secret pledge or secret handshake. If you want to be a Wiccan than you are one. Usually people like to do an initiation ritual on their own in order to feel like they are committing to Wicca but it's not a requirement.

The Law of Threefold Return

The most important principle of Wicca is the Law of Threefold Return. It has many names, and you might see it called other names like the "Law of 3" or "Rule of 3" but no matter what it's called it's the first thing that you learn when you first start studying Wicca.

The Law of Threefold Return is simple. It states that whatever type of energy that you send out will return to you multiplied by three. This is why it's never a good idea to perform negative spells or to try and hurt or manipulate other people through spells. If you send out negative energy by performing a spell to hurt someone or manipulate them that negative energy will come back to you three times as strong as the energy you sent out. That's a lot of negative energy, and no one wants more negative energy in their lives.

The Law of Threefold Return also means that when you send out positive energy it will return you three times stronger, which is why positive spells to create change can be so powerful. If you are familiar with the smash hit The Secret then you already have a pretty good idea of how the Law of 3 works. Whatever you put out you get back, multiplied by three. So when you send out positive energy you will attract even more positive energy which is how you can create the changes that you want to create in your life.

Physics has proven that everything has energy. Tapping into that energy and directing it so that you can attract the money, love, success and other things you want is not bad. It's something that people who want to take control of their lives have done for centuries. And it works.

The Wiccan Rede

There are not a lot of rules in Wicca. It's a religion that celebrates individuality and creativity. But there is one rule that no witch should ever break. Don't do spells to hurt people. It's just that simple. Don't try to hurt someone and don't try to take away a person's free will. If you do, there will be serious consequences because of the Law of Threefold Return. So even though there is no religious organization that will track you down and throw you out of the religion if you do a spell trying to hurt someone you will still send up paying a pretty hefty price for your spell. Don't risk it.

Spells that are designed to take away another person's free will are also not recommended because they can, in some cases, cause harm. For example if someone does a love spell trying to get a specific person to fall in love with them that is taking away someone's free will, and that will cause the witch to face some serious karmic consequences.

When you are creating spells remember that your spells must focus energy that is directed outward but not at any specific person. Don't manipulate others and don't try to cause them physical, mental or emotional harm. As long as you are not actively trying to hurt another person you can cast whatever spells you want.

Sarah Thompson

The God and the Goddess Rule The Universe

Wicca is polytheistic religion, meaning that that Wiccans worship more than one god. In fact, Wicca incorporates the gods and goddesses of many religions. That's because Wiccans believe that all the gods and goddesses worshipped in other religions are just faces of one god and goddess with different names.

Wiccans believe that the Horned God of the Earth and the Moon Goddess are the equal but opposite forces that makeup the Universe. So it doesn't matter what name you give to the Goddess or the God because you are still invoking the male energy of the Universe or the female energy of the Universe. Both are sacred and both need the other one in order for the Universe to stay in balance.

So when you are performing spells, meditating, or praying it doesn't matter what name you give to the Goddess or the God. You can invoke the energy of any god or goddess that you feel is appropriate. If you are performing a spell for love you might want to invoke the energy of Aphrodite, the goddess of love. Or if you are performing a spell to attract money you might want to call upon Cerunnos the Celtic god of money and good fortune.

Gods and Goddesses From All Religions Welcome

Since Wicca was founded on the Ancient Celtic belief system many of the gods and goddesses that are present in Wicca are Celtic, but Wiccans welcome and invoke the deities of other cultures and religions as well. The Celtic deities were based on the Roman deities, who were based on the gods and goddesses worshipped by the Ancient Greeks. And the Ancient Egyptians, Sumerians, and other cultures all had their own pantheons of deities as well. Yet almost all polytheistic religions, or religions that have more than one deity, have the same deities. They just have different names.

So Wicca celebrates the gods and goddesses of other religions and welcomes them into the practice of Wicca. If a witch feels a closeness to an Egyptian goddess she might have a statue of that goddess on her altar. Or a witch who casts a spell for strength might call upon the Roman god of war to give him strength to face a tough situation or a tough job.

Because Wiccans believe that all the gods and goddesses represent the sacred male and female energies of the Universe they respect all religions equally and let people worship whichever gods and goddesses they feel called to worship.

Magic is Real

Magic is really just the focusing and directing of energy and it is absolutely real. When you use spells to do magic you are just tapping into that energy and directing the flow of it. That is how Wiccans use spells and magic work to make change in their lives and in the world.

But it's important to have realistic expectations. The type of magic that you see in movies like Harry Potter or in Disney movies is made up. Real magic is subtle and results in changes that might not occur right away. Always remember that using magic is just focusing and shifting energy patterns. The changes that you are trying to bring about might take time to manifest. That doesn't mean that your spell didn't work and it doesn't mean that magic isn't real.

When you are practicing magic you will need to use tools that will help you focus your mind and focus your energy on the changes that you are trying to bring about. The strength of your focus is what makes the magic happen. You can increase your focus and concentration through practices like meditation.

No Doctrine Required

Most religions have ironclad doctrines that teach followers how the world was created, what happens after they die, and how to be moral and just people while they are alive. Wicca has no doctrine. Wiccans are independent people who like to think for themselves and usually reject doctrine, especially religious doctrine.

Wiccans believe that the Law of Threefold Return makes doctrine unnecessary. As long as you know that whatever energy you put out you will get back times three you can make your down decisions about to act. If you cast spells or try to manipulate others knowing that you will end up getting some very negative energy back in return and you choose to do it anyway then as long as you accept the consequences of your actions the decision is up to you.

Sarah Thompson

Wicca doesn't require followers to seek forgiveness from a priest or anyone else. Wiccans don't believe in heaven or hell so they have no need of priests or other people to intercede for them with an all knowing god. Wiccans believe that everyone is responsible for their own actions.

A Direct Line to the Divine

Most other religions have priests, rabbis, or other intermediaries that act as the go-between people and the Divine. It's the job of the priest or pastor or rabbi to tell you what God's will is and speak to God on your behalf. But Wicca doesn't have pastors or rabbis or anyone else that speaks for the Divine. There are Wiccan priests who serve in covens but they act more as leaders than intermediaries.

That's because Wicca is a very individual religion. You are encouraged to build your own relationship with the Divine and develop your own spirituality. Part of learning to recognize and direct the energy all around you is developing your own understanding of the Universe. Wiccans are encouraged to read, pray, and meditate in order to have a better understanding of the mysteries of the world around them.

There are no Sunday school classes, no weekly church services, and no catechism to be taught or learned. Each witch must study and learn on their own in order to develop a stronger faith and sense of connection to the Universe. If you prefer the company of others you can study with a group, like a coven, but there are many solitary witches that like to study and practice spell work on their own.

Spells Should be Cast In Harmony with the Lunar Cycle

Magic is done according to the lunar cycle. Spells that are done to increase things like love, prosperity, peace and so on should always be done during the full moon or the day just before the full moon. The fullness of the moon will attract abundance, so any spells done to attract good things during the full moon will put out an energy of abundance.

Spells that are done to take away anxiety, take away fear, or decrease stress should be done during the new moon or while the moon is waning. The energy of the moon during this cycle is focused on lessening so the energy of the moon will make the spell more effective. Spells done for spiritual awakening, learning, or divination should always be done only during the new moon.

If you're not sure when you should do a particular spell ask yourself what the real purpose of the spell is. Clarify your intentions and then it should be clear what phase of the moon would help that spell be effective. You can keep track of the moon phases with a Farmer's Almanac or just by checking online. If you have trouble keeping track of the Lunar Cycle you can make yourself a calendar and hang it on the wall so that you will always know when you should perform a certain spell.

Spells Create Change That You Can't Always See
When you think about witches casting spell you probably see an image in your mind of black clad women stirring a steaming large black pot over a fire. Or maybe you think of a witch waving a wand and turning a prince into a frog, or vice versa. But that's Disney magic. Real magic is often very subtle and hard to detect. So you have to be on the lookout for small changes after you cast a spell.

Wicca

When you cast a spell you are directing energy that will create change like the ripples in a pond. The changes that are created often won't be obvious or dramatic. But the spells that you cast will result in events unfolding to give you the opportunity to make huge changes in your life. You have to be paying attention and you have to seize the opportunities.

Often people who are new to Wicca will think that a spell they cast didn't work because they won't be looking for the signs that it did work. For example if you cast a spell to get a new job you probably will not get a call out of the blue from the company you have been dying to work for. But, you might find yourself talking to a stranger at a party or on the train who works at that company and can recommend you for a job to HR department. Or if you want to move up at your current company a job might open up that would be perfect for you.

If you cast a spell for more money a stack of money won't just appear, and the winning lottery numbers probably won't either. But you might find a unique opportunity for a part time income like teaching something that you love. Be ready for all the opportunities that spells will create for you.

Sarah Thompson

Everything Has Energy

Spells work because the Universe and everything in it is made of energy. Energy can be acted upon and directed, which is what spells are for. There is energy all around you. People, animals, plants, even the air has energy.

That's why the air before a storm feels almost electrified and why if someone around you is in a bad mood you will feel upset too. Energy is everywhere and you are interacting with it all the time. Spells are just a tool that you can use to focus energy. By focusing your energy and the energy all around you it's easy to create change and attract the type of positive energy that will change your life for the better.

Energy cannot be created or destroyed. Physics has proven that. So learning how to use the energy that is constantly around you is just a smart way to take control of your life. As long as you are not manipulating people or trying to cause harm to people there is nothing wrong with trying to shift the energy around you to create positive changes. It's a natural process, not something to fear or worry about.

Wicca is simply the practice of learning how to use the energy that is present in the world to get the things that you want and the things that will make your life better.

Respect The Natural World

Respect for nature is an import part of Wicca. The natural world is full of very powerful energy and is the source of life for animals and humans alike. Wiccans believe strongly in protecting and honoring the Earth and the natural world. Many volunteer for groups that work directly to protect the Earth from pollution and destruction.

Natural elements like crystals, stones, water and even dirt can play important roles in casting spells. They can amplify and help direct the energy raised during a spellcasting so that your spells are much more effective. Wiccans feel a kinship with the natural world and try to spend as much time outdoors as possible.

Wicca is regarded as an Earth centered religion because so many of the practices and holidays are related to the cycles and seasons of the Earth. Wiccans try to live very much in tune with the planet.

There are eight major holidays in the Wiccan religion and all of them correspond to the turning of the seasons or other natural events.

In fact, some of the holidays that you probably already celebrate like Halloween, Christmas and Easter started out as Pagan celebrations that represented the turning of the seasons. Wicca has Pagan roots and has borrowed a lot of traditionally Pagan beliefs and practices and built upon them

Magic Tools Make Spells More Effective

True magic is all based on energy, so technically it can be done without any tools at all. But it is really only very skilled and experienced witches who can perform magic without any tools. Tools are very useful, especially for beginners, because they make it much easier to focus your energy and visualize parts of the spell.

There are some basic tools that every witch should have. You don't need to buy all of these at once. Look in thrift shops, garage sales, and other out of the way places and buy tools that speak to you. Or, make your own. It's better to wait and find the perfect tools than it is to buy something off the shelf. The tools that you should have to perform spells include:

Cauldron – this is usually a small iron pot that you can use to mix herbs or place burning items.

Wand – Wands are used for summoning the spirits of the Air and focusing energy. Natural wands made from tree branches are the best.

Incense burner – Incense is a very important part of spellcasting. Even a cheap basic incense burner will do the job but you might want to invest in a nice brass or pottery incense burner down the line.

Chalice- Your chalice can be glass, ceramic, or metallic. Most people use a glass chalice. You can even just use a special piece of glassware. Some people prefer to use ornate carved chalices that are available in Wiccan supply stores.

Altar Cloth – An altar cloth can be any piece of cloth, although most witches prefer pure cotton or silk material. Natural materials are the best to use. An altar cloth is a special cloth only used for spellwork. It can transform any flat surface into a magical surface. You may want to personalize your cloth with embroidery or embellishments.

When you are not using your magical tools they can sit on your altar or you can wrap them in your altar cloth and store them out of sight. This is a good option if you live with other people who don't know about your Wiccan practices.

Spells Are Essential

A lot of people get scared by the idea of casting a spell, but really a spell is just like a prayer to a Wiccan. Instead of praying to a deity to make something happen a witch uses a spell to focus all the energy around them and make things happen. Spells can be just as powerful as prayers, and really are a type of prayer if you think about it.

Spells can be created for just about any purpose. Just don't use spells to hurt or manipulate others. A spell can be a simple two sentence statement or can be a multiple paragraph speech. As long as the Wiccan performing the spell does it with good intentions and clear direction a spell can be powerful even when it's short. In fact sometimes the shortest spells can be the most powerful, if there is a lot of focus behind them.

Saying spells out loud is a good way to focus on what you are doing and what you want to happen as a result. By speaking the words out loud you are announcing what you want to the Universe and putting all your energy out into the world. The ripple effects from that are what make the spell effective.

If necessary you can mutter the words under your breath but spells are better if you can announce them clearly in a powerful tone of voice. Performing spells with others will increase the amount of energy behind the spell and make it even more effective, so if you are casting a spell for something very important it is a good idea to get some of your Wiccan friends together to perform the spell with you.

Write Your Own Spells

When you are just starting to develop your magical practice you might want to use generic spells to get started. But you should write your own spells as soon as possible. When you are writing your own spells you are putting your energy into the words and the spell will be more powerful because it's personal to you and it has your energy in it. Here are some tips for writing spells:

Don't get caught up in the language – Spells don't have to rhyme, although they can if you want them to. They don't have to be full of huge important words either. Don't worry about making it sound poetic or flowery. As long as it comes from your heart that is all that matters.

State your intention clearly – Be very clear about what you are asking for. If you are writing a spell for love then specify what kind of love you want such as a long term romance, a marriage, a life-partner, or a quick but fun fling. If you are writing a spell for better health state clearly the problems that need to be changed like you want to have more energy or you want to be slim again.

Follow the format – Each spell should have the same basic format. The spell should start with a blessing or invocation of the spirits. Then you should state what you want. Then make a small offering and give thanks. Spells don't have to be long but they should all include your thanks at the end.

Write the spell down – Keep your spells in case you need them again. You can always change them or add on to them later if you find that the spell isn't as effective as you want. Eventually you will create your own Book of Shadows to hold all your personal spells.

Magic Works Best Outdoors

It's not always feasible to practice magic and cast spells outdoors, but whenever you can do your magical work outside you should. The natural energy all around you will amplify your spell and make it more effective. There is a fantastic energy that comes from practicing magic at the beach, or in the woods that can't be matched indoors.

But, not everyone lives in a place where the outdoors is private, safe and accessible for witches who want to cast spells outside. If you have to be a strictly indoor witch you can bring the outdoors inside by having lots of live plants and herbs growing in pots in your apartment. Open the windows or the patio door when you perform magic to let in some of the natural air.

You can also bring some tokens of the outdoors inside and keep them on your altar like stones to represent the earth, leaves to represent the natural air, and a pot of salt water to represent the ocean. Another option is to wear jewelry made from sea glass or gems that will put you in touch with the outside world. You can use a natural sounds machine to add the sounds of rain, ocean waves, or birds in the forest to put you in the right frame of mind to cast spells.

Wicca Welcomes Everyone

Wicca is an accepting religion that welcomes everyone regardless of race, age, appearance, experience, sexuality, nationality, or any other factors. Everyone from age 1 to 100 and beyond can become a practicing Wiccan. Wicca is a religion of tolerance and acceptance that celebrates the diversity of people as much as the diversity of life upon the planet.

Wiccan celebrations incorporate the traditions of many different cultures around the globe and throughout history. While most Wiccans stick to Celtic traditions there are plenty who have adapted parts of cultures ranging from Ancient Egyptian to Norse into their practices and celebrations. And that's ok. In fact, those differences are celebrated.

To be a practicing Wiccan you must be willing to accept those that are different from you. Wiccans come from all backgrounds and all walks of life. There are soldiers and military personnel who are Wiccans, schoolteachers and office clerks who are Wiccan, stay at home spouses and parents who are Wiccan and students, farmers, and grocery store clerks who are Wiccan. Wicca is a religion for everyone and anyone who wants to take control of their lives and learn how to use the energy all around them to make their lives better.

Conclusion

Wicca may be something that remains a mystery for a very long time, but after reading this book, hopefully you see this subject and are a lot more informed than you were when you picked it up and began to read it. While many will still not understand the full aspects of what all is associated with Wicca, it is important to note that there is a growing amount of people that are learning more and more about this topic.

Wicca is one of the leading religions that are emerging on a regular basis. While there will always be those that look at this subject as something that is used for harmful purposes, there are those that see it for what it really is, which a form or religion that allows those that do not prescribe to the traditional teachings of Christianity to have something that they can believe in and feel that they are accepted in on a regular basis.

Sarah Thompson

One thing that you can do is look into the subject a little deeper as there are far too many concepts and aspects to cover here. You may be surprised at the things that you discover on your own. The more that you know about this topic, the more educated that you will be should you one day find yourself with a person that is part of Wicca. You will know what they are talking about and can actually carry on a conversation with them.

Wicca

Secret Chapter: Free Bonus – "The New Age Handbook"

Like I promised you before in this small chapter I will give you a free EBook as a gift of mine.

Are you looking for something more out of life? If so, you are not alone. Many people are today and find the solution in the New Age Movement.
The New Age movement adopts ideas from a number of different movements that emphasize spirituality and the spiritual conscious mind. The main idea is to enforce serenity of the mind.

A few years ago I began having major problems with both my career and my personal life. As a result, I was suffering from large amounts of stress that impacted my health. I knew I needed to find a way to empower myself but I just couldn't seem to do it. As time went on, the stress became worse and so did my health.

I knew I had to do something.

That's when I decided I had to find a way to improve my life. I knew I owed it to myself and my family to get a handle on this once and for all!

What I discovered completely changed my life!

How did I do it?

I would love to share my secrets with you and my new special report on New Age does just that!

Click here to download the book for free.

Sarah Thompson

Alternatively you can check out this link: https://mjgpublishing.leadpages.net/sarahthompson/

Preview Of 'Tarot: The Ultimate Beginners Guide for Learning the Secrets of Tarot Cards'

Chapter 1 – Finding a Deck

Choosing a Deck of Cards

There are several different decks you can choose from when it comes to tarot cards, and which deck you choose will determine which craft you learn. The most important step in starting your journey to becoming a tarot card reader is to choose the deck of cards you will be working with wisely. You can always change the deck you're working with, so starting out with an easier to learn deck is probably going to be better.

There are several steps you need to take in order to find the right deck for you. I'm going to state this right off the bat, you don't want to choose a tarot card deck on the internet. Do not order one through the mail, the internet, or any other method that doesn't allow you to see and touch the cards.

That's because the first step you're going to take when you choose a tarot card deck is to go to a brick and mortar store and pick them up. You want to get the weight and feel of them in your hands. You're going to want to shuffle them and move them around in order to get an energy connection with them, and then you'll know when you find the right deck of cards. Most people are going to tell you the Rider-Waite deck is the best one to choose for beginners, but that's not always the case.

Once you've felt them, take a long, hard look at them. You want to be sure you have a pleasant visceral reaction to them because you're going to be looking at them a lot. Plus, the visuals you have will aid you when you first start out.

Now that you've picked your tarot card deck, you'll want to count the cards to be sure you're actually holding a tarot card deck and not something that just labeled as such. There should be seventy-eight cards. More or less and it's not a tarot card deck.

If you're planning to do spiritual readings for others, you might want to get a second deck of cards. Each person who touches your cards will leave a spiritual reading, and you'll want your cards that you use for personal readings and practice to only have your energy on them. Therefore, while you're at the store, pick up a second deck of cards you'd like to use for others if you feel you're going to have the chance.

There is one more important think you must remember at choosing a deck of cards. You may be in the store one day and a deck calls out to you. Don't ignore it. You're going to change decks of cards throughout your lifetime and it might just be the time to change. You'll know when you need to change your cards.

Click here to check out the rest of Tarot: The Ultimate Beginners Guide for Learning the Secrets of Tarot Cards on Amazon.

Or go to: http://amzn.to/1HaNty5

Sarah Thompson

Check Out My Other Books

Below you'll find some of my other popular books that are popular on Amazon and Kindle as well. Simply click on the links below to check them out. Alternatively, you can visit my author page on Amazon to see other work done by me.

[My Other Book 'Tarot: The Ultimate Beginners Guide for Learning the Secrets of Tarot Cards'- This Is My Other Book On Amazon](#)

['Tarot: The Advanced Guide for Learning the Secrets of Tarot Cards'](#)

['Manifesting: The Complete Guide to the Law of Attraction to 'Manifest' the Life You Want'](#)

['Wicca: The Ultimate Beginner's Guide to Learning Spells & Witchcraft'](#)

Sarah Thompson

'The Ultimate Guide to Breaking Up: How to Break Up Gracefully and Move On'

If the links do not work, for whatever reason, you can simply search for these titles on the Amazon website to find them.

Made in the USA
Middletown, DE
16 February 2017